W9-CJD-902

GREEK
MYTHOLOGY

SIMONE PAYMENT

rosen
central™

The Rosen Publishing Group, Inc., New York

The author would like to thank Marina Lang for her helpful feedback on the manuscript.

Published in 2006 by The Rosen Publishing Group, Inc.
29 East 21st Street, New York, NY 10010

Library of Congress Cataloging-in-Publication Data

Payment, Simone.
Greek mythology / Simone Payment.
    p. cm.—(Mythology around the world)
Includes bibliographical references.
ISBN 1-4042-0771-6 (lib. bdg.)
1. Mythology, Greek.
I. Title. II. Series.
BL783.P39 2005
292.1'3—dc22

                                        2005014590

Manufactured in the United States of America

On the cover: Sixth-century-BC Greek krater illustrating the Trojan War.

CONTENTS

INTRODUCTION

Many cultures have stories that have been passed down through the ages. These stories—called myths—are tales of gods and goddesses, monsters, and adventure. The myths from ancient Greece may be the best known of all cultures' mythologies, and perhaps the most exciting. The myths of the Greeks, which have been told for thousands of years, are still enjoyed today.

What we call classical Greece (from the sixth to the fourth centuries BC) gave future civilizations more than just stories. The ancient Greeks made huge contributions to modern culture in Greece

The Parthenon, shown here, was the chief temple of the Greek goddess Athena. It was built in the fifth century BC.

and elsewhere. In fact, ancient Greece is often called the cradle of Western civilization. This is because so much of modern life is based on contributions from the Greeks. The United States' current system of government, democracy, came from Greek civilization. The Olympics began in ancient Greece. Great Greek thinkers made revolutionary discoveries in astronomy, biology, and medicine. Ancient Greeks also wrote stories and plays that are still read and performed today. Their art and architecture also live on in modern times.

Ancient Greece was not in the exact location where Greece is today. It included parts of what are now Turkey and Italy. There were dense forests and steep, rocky cliffs along the coast. Inland, there were snow-covered mountains. Many islands dotted the Aegean Sea off the eastern coast of Greece.

In the earliest days of Greece, the country was divided into small, individually governed areas called city-states. City-states were often separated by forests or mountains and were far apart, and the dialects spoken in each city-state varied. Because of these barriers, people did not travel much, so city-states did not frequently interact. If you were born in a particular city-state, you would usually live there your whole life. As a result, each city-state had its own myths that most residents knew and told over and over again.

Starting in the fourth century BC, Alexander the Great (the king of Macedon, a part of Greece) began invading other countries. His successes brought Greeks together politically. Some city-states began to work together, sometimes against a common enemy. By that time, they also shared a common language. People began to travel and move to other city-states. They also began to travel outside of Greece. This travel helped spread Greek myths around the country and to other countries.

Everyday life was not always easy in ancient Greece. People did not live as long as they do now. Life was more difficult, with no modern conveniences such as heat or running water. People had to kill animals and farm for food. The hardships in their daily lives led the ancient Greeks to look to their gods and goddesses for help. They believed that the immortal gods and goddesses had a great deal of power. The gods and goddesses could be helpful to humans if the humans showed them the proper respect. To show respect to the gods and goddesses, Greeks worshipped at their local temples. They wanted to stay in good favor with the higher powers for fear that they might be punished. They also believed that the gods and goddesses might punish not just them but their whole community.

In addition to regular visits to local temples, Greeks also held special festivals to honor specific gods or goddesses. As we will learn later in this book, each god and goddess worshipped by the Greeks played a specific role in life.

1 WHAT ARE MYTHS?

The simplest answer to the question of the chapter title is that a myth is a story. The word "myth" comes from the Greek word *mythos*, which literally means "story." However, myths were much more than simple stories to the Greeks. They were an important part of Greek life. They were passed from person to person and from generation to generation.

Myths tell several types of stories. Some are tales of adventure based on actual events. For example, Homer's *The Iliad* is based on the Trojan War, a ten-year war between the Greeks and the people of the Turkish city of Troy.

This fifth-century-BC terra-cotta carving is of the Greek sea monster Scylla.

This 1757 Italian fresco is a scene from one of the most famous Greek epic poems, *The Iliad*, Homer's epic retelling of the Trojan War. In this scene, Athena *(right)*, the Greek goddess of war, prevents Achilles *(center)*, the great Greek warrior, from killing Agamemnon, king of Mycenae.

Myths were more than just accounts of exciting occurrences. They also told stories about such monumental events as the creation of human beings. In ancient Greece, there was no one text, such as the Bible or the Koran, to explain everything about a particular religion's view of the world. Instead, myths served the purpose of providing answers.

Myths also taught important lessons. For example, they might have warned against being too proud. One version of the Greek myth of Arachne tells how Arachne was turned into a spider for bragging about her weaving skills.

The ancient Greeks also created myths to help them make sense of natural phenomena that they could explain in no other way. For example, the Greeks did not understand why earthquakes occurred. A story about the god Poseidon punishing his enemies by shaking the ground underneath them offered Greeks an answer. Poseidon was also believed to control the sea. His changing moods could explain why the sea was calm one day and stormy the next.

Different Cultures, Similar Myths

If you study ancient cultures, you can see that many of them have myths. Myths are often similar from culture to culture. This is most likely because there are certain qualities of life that are important or meaningful to people everywhere.

Each culture creates myths that reflect its beliefs, which

In Greek mythology, Poseidon, shown here in this fifth-century-BC bronze bust, was the god of the sea, or water, as well as of earthquakes. Partial evidence of the latter is that the name Poseidon means "husband of earth" or "lord of the earth."

Common among most, if not all, mythologies is the notion that the gods and goddesses lived high above the earth, either upon mountaintops or in the sky. The Greek manifestation of this was Mount Olympus, shown here, which was home of the Greek gods and goddesses, who are depicted in the inset painting.

are often a result of its circumstances. For example, myths may be influenced by the geography of the country in which a civilization lives. Mount Olympus, a towering, snow-covered mountain in Greece, became known as the home of the gods in Greek mythology. The top of the mountain was so high and so unreachable to the Greeks that they said the gods and goddesses must live there. Myths are also personalized by what is important to a particular country or culture.

How Myths Spread

Many of the Greek myths were based on people and events from even earlier times. In the very early days of Greece (about 2000 BC), Greeks had huge fleets of ships and attacked neighboring countries. About 1,000 years later, Greece had entered a less heroic era. People

One of the most famous Greek poets, as well as one of the most influential poets of all time, was Homer. Homer lived in either the eighth or the ninth century BC. He authored *The Iliad*, the epic recounting of the Trojan War, and *The Odyssey*, the account of the Trojan War hero Odysseus's journey home.

were poor and life was hard, so they told stories of a more exciting time. Men called bards (poets or story-tellers) would memorize the stories and then travel around the country-side, telling these tales. During the time when each city-state was isolated from the others, stories varied. Bards might change the story slightly, adding their own exciting details.

Eventually, myths were written down in a format similar to a poem. Some of the myths, when written down, were up to 1,000 lines long. Homer (circa eighth or ninth century BC) was one of the most famous bards. He wrote two landmark works, *The Iliad* and *The Odyssey*. *The Iliad* tells the story of the Trojan War. *The Odyssey* tells the many adventures of the Greek hero Odysseus. Two other famous written myths are *Theogony* and *Works and Days* by Hesiod (circa 800 BC). *Theogony* is the story of the creation of the gods. *Works and Days* offers advice on how to farm or on which days to do

WORKS and DAYS.

BOOK I.

SING, Muses, sing, from the *Pierian* Grove;

Begin the Song, and let the Theme be *Jove*;

From him ye sprung, and him ye first should praise;

From your immortal Sire deduce your Lays;

To him alone, to his great Will, we owe,

That we exist, and what we are, below.

Whether we blaze among the Sons of Fame,

Or live obscurely, and without a Name;

G 2 Or

Hesiod *(below)* was the most influential Greek poet in terms of the origin of the Greek gods and goddesses, which he wrote about in *Theogony* and *Works and Days (above)*.

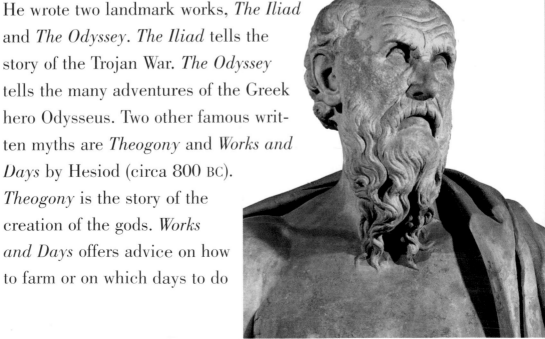

It is thanks to Greek artwork, such as this Greek krater, or wine vase, that we know as much as we do about Greek mythology. This krater depicts the destruction of Troy, one of the most referenced stories in all of Greek mythology.

certain things, like cut your fingernails. Also included in *Works and Days* are myths, such as the story of Pandora, which you will learn about later in this book.

Greeks heard myths at an early age. Elders would tell the stories to young children. Sometimes the stories were used as warnings to get children to behave. Young children also learned about myths at school, although in most places in ancient Greece, only boys went to school.

Adults heard myths at social gatherings and informal meetings. Myths were also recited as a part of rituals at religious temples. In addition, bards might tell myths—or even sing them—for wealthy people or kings. The theater was an important part of Greek life, and sometimes choirs would perform myths as plays.

How Do We Know About Greek Myths?

Greek myths have been passed down for thousands of years. There are several ways we have learned about them. One is through written works, such as books or plays, that were created by later cultures based on stories from ancient Greece. These works have survived and are still enjoyed today. We have also learned about ancient Greek myths through artwork such as sculptures and paintings. The Greeks sometimes told their myths in the form of art, for example creating a sculpture of Zeus or a painting of Aphrodite. Sometimes they made mosaics depicting important myths. They also decorated vases and other containers with stories of their heroes, heroines, gods, and goddesses. Even Greek coins were often decorated with images from myths. Many Greek sculptures still exist today in museums. We can even see some floor mosaics in their original locations. Hopefully, these relics will be preserved for years to come.

2 THE CATEGORIES OF GREEK MYTHS

Myths tell many different types of stories. They can tell us about how life came to be the way it is now. A myth might also explain events such as death or why the seasons change. However, as we mentioned in the previous chapter, myths were sometimes similar across cultures. This could be because ancient people from all around the world were trying to find explanations for things they just could not account for in any other way.

The Creation of Gods and the Universe

One mystery ancient people may have tried to explain is how the

This sixth-century-BC Laconian-style bowl illustrates the Greek god Zeus with an eagle.

universe was created. The poet Hesiod wrote down the first attempt to answer this question in his work *Theogony*. According to *Theogony*, in the beginning there was Chaos, which was a dark, swirling void. Eventually, things began to emerge from Chaos, such as Gaea (Earth), Uranus (sky), and Tartarus (the dark place under Earth). Gaea and Uranus came together to form several monsters, including the Cyclopes, who had one eye in the middle of their foreheads. Gaea and Uranus also produced twelve Titans, who were humanlike creatures.

The twelve Titans ruled the universe, some taking charge of the sea, others of the sun or the moon. Eventually, two of them, Rhea and Cronus, married and together they had six children. As each of the first five was born, Cronus swallowed them. He alone wanted to rule the world, and he didn't want competition from his children. Rhea was greatly upset by this, so when Zeus, the sixth child, was born, she hid him in a cave. To fool Cronus, she gave him a rock wrapped in cloth. Cronus grabbed it and swallowed it whole, thinking it was his child.

Zeus grew up and eventually learned about his brothers and sisters whom Cronus had swallowed. He wanted to set them free. His grandmother, Gaea, helped Zeus give Cronus a strong medicine to make him throw up. Out came the stone and Zeus's five brothers and sisters: Hestia, Demeter, Hera, Hades, and Poseidon.

Zeus led his five brothers and sisters in a ten-year battle against Cronus and the other Titans. Eventually, two of the Titans (Prometheus and his brother Epimetheus) decided to help Zeus.

This detail from the base of a second-century-AD marble statue illustrates the myth of Rhea and Cronus. True to the story, Rhea *(left)* hands Cronus what he believes is Zeus. As with his other children, Cronus swallows what is handed to him, not knowing that what Rhea handed him was not his child, but a stone wrapped in cloth.

They advised him to unleash the Cyclopes and other monsters from Tartarus. Zeus knew immediately that this was a good idea. The Cyclopes were so happy to be free that they gave Zeus gifts of thunder and lightning. They gave Hades a hat that would make him invisible. Poseidon got a three-pronged spear. After a long fierce battle, Zeus and his allies won. They sent the Titans to Tartarus and began their rule of the universe.

The Creation of the Human Race

In Greek mythology, the creation of humans was a slow, gradual process. The ancient Greeks believed that Cronus created the first humans. They were called the Golden Race and they lived easy, perfect lives. The Golden Race eventually died out but continued to watch over the next race. They were called the Race of Silver, but they were childish and fought a great deal. Zeus, who was by then ruling the universe, got tired of them. He decided to create a new race from ash trees. These new humans were very aggressive. They were devoted to Ares, the god of war. They were called the Race of Bronze because they made their weapons from that metal. Eventually, they killed each other off with their constant fighting.

The Greek goddess Hera, depicted here in this sixth-century-BC stone bust, is a recurring character in Greek mythology. In addition to being Zeus's sister, Hera was also Zeus's wife. She is often characterized as overcome by jealousy because of Zeus's numerous romantic engagements.

The next race was called Heroes. Also created by Zeus, they fought a lot, too, and eventually were replaced by the current human race. This race was known as the Race of Iron. The ancient Greeks believed that the Race of Iron was imperfect, as humans are imperfect, and that in the future things would only get worse.

The Flood

Many ancient religions and cultures had stories of a great flood. The ancient Greeks were no exception. In their myths, a great

This engraving is from Ovid's *Metamorphosis* and depicts the myth of Deukalion and Pyrrha. Illustrated is the flood, which wiped out everyone except Deukalion and Pyrrha, who were saved.

flood wiped out the people of the Bronze Age (although some stories say that they had killed each other off before the flood). Most stories say that there were two survivors of the great flood: Deukalion and his wife, Pyrrha. They had survived because Deukalion had built a wooden chest. In it he and his wife sailed on the rising waters for nine days and nights. Eventually, they reached Mount Parnassus.

To thank Zeus for sparing them, they made sacrifices to him. Zeus rewarded them by letting Deukalion and Pyrrha create a new race of people to inhabit Earth. To do this, they threw stones over their heads. When the stones landed, the ones Deukalion had thrown became men; Pyrrha's became women.

Apollo is shown here mourning the death of Hyakinthos, whose life he unintentionally ended when he hit him in the head with a discus. According to legend, Apollo and Hyakinthos were lovers. However, the god Zephyrus was also in love with Hyakinthos, and out of jealousy, he allowed the discus to strike and kill him.

Death and Rebirth

Other phenomena the Greeks explained through their myths were death and rebirth. In many Greek myths, a person dies but is reborn in another form. One such myth is the story of Hyakinthos.

21

Demeter here mourns for her daughter, Persephone, after Persephone is stolen away by Hades to the underworld. The legend states that crops stop growing for four months each year while Persephone is in the underworld, explaining why Greek fields are barren after harvesttime.

Hyakinthos was a boy who was friends with the god Apollo. Both liked sports, and one day they were playing with a discus. Apollo threw the discus and hit Hyakinthos in the head by accident, killing him. Apollo was extremely upset by the death of his friend.

Some versions of this story suggest that Apollo brought his friend back to life. Most versions say that Hyakinthos's blood on the ground formed a beautiful flower that comes back every spring. This flower, which we know as the hyacinth, still grows in modern times.

Seasons

The ancient Greeks used the myth of Demeter and Persephone to explain the changing of the seasons. Demeter, the goddess of corn and fertility, had a daughter named Persephone. Hades, the god of the underworld, kidnapped Persephone and brought her to live in the underworld with him. Not knowing what had happened to her daughter, Demeter looked everywhere for Persephone. She wandered Earth, but was unable to find her daughter. Finally, she went into a temple and stayed there. While she was in the temple, crops all over the world stopped growing. Zeus realized this was a huge problem, so he ordered his brother Hades to send Persephone back to her mother.

But Hades would only allow Persephone to live with her mother for part of the year. Before Persephone left the underworld, Hades gave her four pomegranate seeds. By eating them, she was required to spend four months of the year in the underworld. During the four months of every year she spent with Hades, Demeter was in mourning and no crops would grow. Then, when Persephone emerged from the underworld, plants and crops would bloom again.

3 GREEK GODS AND GODDESSES

In some ways, the gods and goddesses were very much like people. They usually had humanlike bodies, although they were much larger and stronger than humans. They also had human feelings such as jealousy and vengefulness. The fact that the gods and goddesses were similar to humans was unusual. Earlier cultures and people in other parts of the world worshipped gods and goddesses that were unlike humans in almost every way. In some cultures and religions, gods and goddesses took the form of animals. In others, such as in Christianity, God could not be explained in human terms at all. The fact that the ancient Greeks created some other gods and goddesses in their own image may have been because some of the stories they told were loosely based on real-life people and events from their past.

Of course, in many other ways, gods and goddesses were not at all like humans. They were extremely powerful and were able to do things no human could. They had supernatural powers, such as the ability to turn a man into an animal.

This Greek carving, titled
Exaltation of the Flower, **is from the fifth century** BC.

In Homer's *The Odyssey*, the hero, Odysseus, journeys home from Troy to Ithaca. On his way, he encounters the Sirens, beautiful temptresses who lure Odysseus and his crew to the dangerously rocky shore, as depicted in this third-century-AD mosaic.

Most of the gods lived on Mount Olympus, which is an actual mountain in central Greece. The gods and goddesses lived an easy, pleasant life there. They knew they were not going to die, so they were in no rush to do anything. They never had to worry about food or shelter. In *The Odyssey*, Homer describes Mount Olympus in this way: "It is not shaken by winds or drenched with rain nor do snowstorms assail it, but always brightness is spread about it, without clouds, and a clear light plays about it." However, despite their easy life on Mount Olympus, the gods and goddesses were very competitive. They fought with each other often, and could be cruel and nasty. They were jealous of each other, and each wanted to be more powerful than the others.

The Roles of Gods and Goddesses

The ancient Greeks worshipped many gods and goddesses, who served many functions for the Greeks. The Greeks looked to them for guidance. For example, the god Apollo was associated with music, so musicians would make special offerings to him.

A god might represent a part of nature, as Poseidon did the sea. Sailors would ask Poseidon for help on their journeys. The goddess Athena was associated with wisdom, and Aphrodite with love. A god or goddess might also be identified with a particular city-state, as Athena was with Athens.

Gods and goddesses could help humans—if they felt like it— by giving them special powers or tools. This is known as divine intervention. Usually, gods and goddesses didn't bother getting involved with humans. In general, they would intervene in human affairs only when it served a particular purpose for them. They often used humans to enact revenge against another god or goddess.

When gods and goddesses interacted with humans, it was only in certain ways. The humans always had to remember their place, which was beneath the gods or goddesses in terms of power. Any humans who didn't were punished.

Olympian Gods and Goddesses

There are different ways to classify the gods and goddesses, but one of the easiest ways is to divide them into those who lived on Mount Olympus, and those who lived elsewhere.

Zeus and Hera

Zeus and Hera ruled as king and queen of the gods and goddesses. Zeus controlled the weather and the sky, and was also the god of hospitality. Although he was married to Hera, Zeus had a weakness for falling in love with human women.

Zeus, characterized in this stone carving holding Ganymede, was the supreme ruler over Mount Olympus and over the entire Greek pantheon. Zeus was a prominent figure in both Homer's *The Iliad* and Hesoid's *Theogony*.

This made Hera incredibly jealous, and she often took her jealousy and anger out on the women Zeus loved, or on his children born to other women.

Poseidon

Zeus's brother Poseidon was a powerful god. He ruled the sea and could also use his great force to shake the ground, causing earthquakes.

Hephaestus and Aphrodite

Hephaestus was the god of metalworkers and craftsmen. Hera was his mother and in some myths Zeus was his father. Other myths say he has no father. He walked with a limp, and the other gods and goddesses sometimes made fun of him. However, he built beautiful palaces on Mount Olympus and they respected his skills with metal and fire. Aphrodite was the goddess of love and beauty and was married to Hephaestus. There are conflicting stories about how Aphrodite was born. *Theogony* says that she was created when drops of Uranus's blood fell on the ocean. However, *The Iliad* says she was the daughter of Zeus and Dione.

Hermes

Hermes was a god with many roles. He was the messenger for the other gods, and he brought souls to Hades, the god of the underworld. Hermes was also the god of

Hephaestus, shown in this third-century-BC statuette, was the Greek god of fire, particularly the fire of metalworkers. One myth recounts how he was born crippled. At the sight of him, his mother, Hera, threw him off Mount Olympus. He fell for a day and landed in the sea, where he was rescued by nymphs.

This first-century-AD marble sculpture shows Apollo playing the zither, an instrument similar to a harp. Apollo was the most respected and influential of all the Greek gods, but his nature was also the most obscure. He had many functions, and from the time of Homer onward, he was a god of complexity and intrigue.

fertility, herds, and of thieves. He was born to Maia, a nymph, and his father was Zeus.

Ares and Athena

The god of war, Ares, was the son of Zeus and Hera. The goddess of war was Athena. She was also the goddess of wisdom and household arts (especially weaving and spinning). Athena was the

29

daughter of Zeus and Metis, a human woman. She was born not from Metis's body, however, but fully formed from Zeus's head when it was split open by Hephaestus.

Apollo and Artemis

Apollo ruled over the sun, poetry, music, and prophecy. He was also a healer and he liked to restore order. He was the son of Zeus and the goddess Leto. Apollo's twin, Artemis, was the goddess of the moon. She was a huntress and the mistress of wild animals. Artemis also looked after unmarried girls and was the goddess of childbirth.

Demeter

The goddess of grain, harvests, and fertility was Demeter. Demeter was the sister of Zeus and the mother of Persephone, who later ruled the underworld.

Hestia and Dionysus

Zeus's sister Hestia was the goddess of hearth and home. She was an original resident of Mount Olympus, but was later replaced by Dionysus, the god of wine. Dionysus had an interesting birth. His mortal mother, Semele, gave birth to him prematurely (due to some interference from the jealous Hera). His father, Zeus, stuffed the infant Dionysus into his thigh until he was ready to be born. Dionysus is sometimes referred to as "twice born" because of this.

This 1865 painting depicts the Greek princess Psyche in the underworld, the ugliness of which sits in stark contrast with her beauty. There are versions of the underworld across many mythologies. Each is often similar to the rest in that it is usually reached by crossing a river and entered by passing a guard. Cerberus was the guard in Greek mythology.

Underworld Gods and Goddesses

Zeus's brother Hades was the god of the underworld. Hades was lonely ruling the underworld, so Zeus helped him kidnap Persephone, Demeter's daughter. Persephone became the queen of the underworld. The goddess Hecate also lived in the underworld. She was known as the goddess of night or darkness, but also defended children and performed other good deeds.

Other Gods and Goddesses

Greek myths contained a few other kinds of gods. These were sometimes called minor gods because they did not play as important a role in the myths as did the gods and goddesses who lived on Mount Olympus or in the underworld.

The nymphs were one type of minor god. They were female nature spirits and they lived in the forests, woods, rivers, seas, and clouds. They interacted with the gods and with humans.

Some gods lived in the forests, sky, or sea. Forest gods included Pan and the centaurs. Pan was half goat and half man. The centaurs were half man, half horse. Zephyr (the warm, gentle, west wind) and Boreas (the stormy north wind) were sky gods. One of the sea gods was Proteus, who was able to change his shape. He could change himself into any number of forms, such as that of an animal or even a tree. Another sea god, named Phorcys, ruled over sea animals such as seals and sea lions.

4 GREEK HEROES AND HEROINES

As we have discussed, humans sometimes interacted with the gods. This was made easy by the fact that gods had human-like forms, although the gods were larger and more powerful. The Greeks believed that heroes and heroines were somewhere between gods and humans. Heroes and heroines were not as powerful as the gods. However, they were stronger in many ways than humans. Heroes and heroines were also sometimes the sons or daughters of gods, which contributed to the idea that they were halfway between gods and humans.

Just as myths are some-times similar in many different cultures,

This third- or second-century-BC statuette is of the Greek female athlete Atalanta.

heroes and heroines are often similar from culture to culture. Many of the Greek heroes and heroines share characteristics with heroes and heroines from other cultures and other times. For example, in most tales, heroes and heroines battle against some kind of danger or difficulty. In the end, the hero or heroine is victorious. Their victory usually helps the rest of society in some way.

Heracles

One of the most famous heroes of ancient Greece, or perhaps any time, is Heracles. (Heracles is better known by his Roman name, Hercules.) The son of Zeus and a human woman (Alkmene), Heracles was the strongest man in Greece. However, he was not perfect. He had a very bad temper and was not as smart as other Greek heroes. His temper got him into a lot of trouble, and it led to what he is most famous for: his twelve labors.

Heracles, depicted here in this first-century-AD marble bust, is among the most famous Greek gods. Some scholars believe that this mythological figure may have been based on a real man, who was likely a chieftain or vassal from the kingdom of Argos.

Hera, jealous that Heracles was Zeus's son with another woman, always disliked Heracles. One day she made him temporarily insane, and he killed his family while under her spell. When he came to his senses, he was ashamed and terribly upset. He wanted to kill himself, but before he did, he went to the Temple of Apollo at Delphi, in central Greece, for advice.

There he talked to the oracle, a priestess who was believed to be in direct communication with Apollo. The oracle gave advice to humans based on information from Apollo. She told Heracles that if he completed twelve difficult tasks, he would be able to forgive himself. His tasks included capturing or killing monsters such as the Hydra (which had a huge body and nine heads) and Cerberus (the three-headed dog that guarded the underworld).

Even though it took Heracles years to accomplish his twelve labors, he did finish them and was finally able to forgive himself. He completed many other heroic tasks in his lifetime, and eventually the gods made him immortal.

Atalanta

Atalanta was a heroine well known for her bravery and hunting skills. Abandoned in the woods by her father, Atalanta was raised by a bear. She was always comfortable in nature and, like the goddess Artemis, was a fearless hunter. An oracle had told Atalanta that she should not marry, so she made a plan to avoid marriage. If a man proposed to her, she would challenge him to a race. If he won, they would marry, but if he lost, she would kill him.

This fifteenth-century Persian rendition of the myth of Atalanta shows Atalanta and Melanion racing. According to the myth, Melanion must win the race to secure Atalanta's hand in marriage. With the aid of Aphrodite, he dropped golden apples in front of her so that she picked them up and lost the race.

Many men lost this challenge until Melanion decided to ask Aphrodite for help in winning the race. Aphrodite gave Melanion golden apples, and during the race Melanion dropped them in front of Atalanta. Stopping to pick them up, Atalanta lost the race and she and Melanion were married. However, they did not live happily ever after. They broke one of Zeus's rules, and, in one version, he punished them by turning them into lions.

Theseus and Ariadne

Theseus is another famous Greek hero. There are many stories told about his adventures. One of the most famous is the tale of how he defeated the Minotaur with the help of Ariadne.

The Minotaur was a monster that lived trapped in a giant maze on the island of Crete. It had the body of a man, but the head and tail of a bull. Every nine years, seven boys and seven girls were sent into the maze as a sacrifice. No one knew exactly what happened to sacrifices in the maze. They were not allowed to take any weapons or other protection into the maze. Most people assumed the Minotaur ate them.

When Theseus heard about this, he wanted to kill the Minotaur to prevent more deaths. He volunteered to go to the island of Crete as one of the sacrifices. On the island, he met Ariadne, the daughter of the king of Crete. Ariadne fell in love with Theseus and wanted to help him kill the Minotaur.

To do this, she gave him a bronze sword, even though the sacrifices weren't supposed to enter the maze with weapons. The

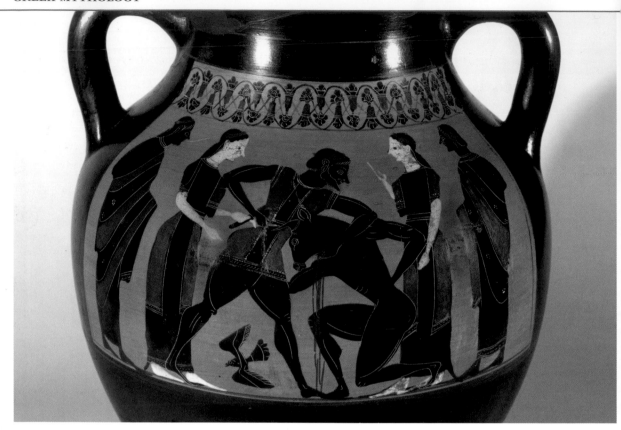

The myth of Theseus and Ariadne is among the most popular in Greek mythology. Here is a scene from that myth on a sixth-century-BC piece of Greek pottery. Theseus is shown slaying the Minotaur. Standing around them are the saved seven boys and seven girls who were destined to be sacrificed.

other tool she gave Theseus was a ball of thread. Ariadne told Theseus to tie one end of the thread to a pillar near the entrance of the maze. As he crept through the maze, he unwound the thread. At last, he reached the sleeping Minotaur and killed the beast. Finding his way back out of the maze afterward might have been difficult, but he was able to follow the trail of the thread Ariadne had given him. In this way, he made it back to the entrance. Theseus and Ariadne then left the island with the young men and women who would have been killed by the Minotaur if it were not for Theseus's bravery.

The Heroes and Heroines of the Trojan War

The Trojan War is the focus of many exciting myths. The war began as a result of the jealousy and competitiveness of the gods and goddesses. The meddling of the gods resulted in a war between Greece and the city of Troy. The war raged for ten years. Many interesting heroes and heroines played a part in the war, and many lost their lives. Others rose as heroes. *The Iliad* tells about the exciting events of the Trojan War.

One of the great heroes of the Trojan War was Achilles. He was a brave warrior who led the Greeks in the Trojan War. Achilles killed Hector, the greatest Trojan hero. With Hector dead, the Trojans needed all the help they could get. Penthesilea, an Amazon queen, assisted the Trojans. She battled bravely, but she, too, was killed by Achilles.

Another Greek warrior who fought in the Trojan War was Odysseus, who was a Greek king. *The Odyssey* tells the story of his ten-year journey home after the war. During his travels, he overcomes many monsters and other obstacles.

5 THE GREEK MYTHS

Did you ever see a shooting star and wonder what it was? Did you ever think about why a spider spins a web or how we learned about fire? The Greeks did. Without good explanations for any of those things, they invented myths to provide some creative answers.

Did your parents ever tell you a story about what might happen to you if you disobeyed them? Elders in ancient Greece told such stories, and they had plenty of exciting myths to choose from.

Do you enjoy stories of battles and daring adventure? So did the Greeks. As we learned before, there are many types of Greek myths. The six myths that follow provide some examples.

Narcissus

The story of Narcissus is among the most popular Greek myths. The message the story of Narcissus

This sixth-century-AD Etruscan bowl depicts an eagle picking out Prometheus's liver.

The myth of Narcissus is one of the most popular from the Greeks and still resonates in contemporary times. This sixteenth- or seventeenth-century painting, titled *Narcissus at the Pool*, characterizes the young man as a figure obsessed with his own beauty, fated to pine away beside the water that bears his reflection.

gave to the Greeks, as well as to readers today, is that vanity, or love of oneself, is a destructive trait. The Greeks were even superstitious of looking at one's own reflection, believing that doing such could result in bad luck or even death. The contemporary English word "narcissism," meaning "egoism" or "love of one's own body," even derives from this powerful Greek myth, and is most often spoken with a negative connotation. Specifically, the word comes from the Greek word *narke*, which means "numb," or being insensitive to others. Interestingly enough, the English word "narcotic," or illegal drug, also derives from the same Greek word.

Narcissus, a hero of the territory of Thespiae in Boeotia, was the son of the river god Cephissus and the nymph Leiriope. He was a beautiful young man who was to have a long life if he never looked at his own reflection. All the while, young girls and nymphs fell in love with his beauty. Narcissus, however, rejected each of their advances, even those of the nymph Echo. Echo was so distraught over Narcissus's rejection of her that she eventually pined, or faded, away into nothing but a whisper.

Nemesis, the Greek goddess of divine justice, learned about Narcissus's rejection of Echo. As punishment, she led Narcissus to fall in love with his own reflection. This he did, staring day and night into his own image in the waters of a pond until he faded away.

There are several versions of the story of Narcissus, some of which have been adapted into Roman mythology. In one version, the reason why Narcissus gazes at his own reflection is not for the love of himself, but for that of his late twin sister, whom he adored and whose appearance he sought in his own reflection. This version adds a powerful new dimension to the myth. The moral of the story is no longer the harm in loving one's self. Instead, this version teaches us that we do harm by obsessing over others, or even that which we cannot obtain.

In yet another version, a young man named Ameinias was in love with Narcissus. Narcissus scorned his love by giving Ameinias the present of a sword, a symbol of rejection. Ameinias used the sword to take his own life while asking Nemesis to teach Narcissus about the pain of unrequited love. Nemesis did so by letting Narcissus become enamored with his own beauty.

Prometheus

The story of Prometheus was an alternative to the story of creation of humans told by Hesiod in *Works and Days*, as previously mentioned. In this version, Prometheus, one of the Titans, was given his freedom after the war between Zeus and the Titans.

This painting by Peter Paul Reubens is titled *Prometheus Bound* and depicts the myth of Prometheus as told by the Greek dramatist Aeschylus. An eagle is picking out Prometheus's liver. The apparent meaning of Prometheus's name is "forethinker," as he was known for being both smart and crafty.

Prometheus was very smart and Zeus admired his wisdom. So, Zeus allowed Prometheus and his brother Epimetheus to create humans and animals. Epimetheus (whose name means "afterthought") was not as smart as his brother. He gave all kinds of protection—like fur, wings, and shells—to the animals. There was nothing left for humans, so when Prometheus created humans from dirt and water, they had no protection.

Prometheus felt sorry for humans and wanted to give them the gift of fire. Zeus was very opposed to this. He didn't feel humans were worthy of something as useful and wonderful as fire. Prometheus decided to disobey Zeus and he stole some fire from the sun. He taught the humans he had created how to use fire to cook and stay warm. Prometheus also taught them how to use fire to create weapons made of metal.

When Zeus discovered Prometheus's betrayal, he decided he must punish Prometheus and the humans. To punish Prometheus, Zeus had Hephaestus, the god of metalworkers, chain Prometheus to a rock high in the mountains. Prometheus remained chained to the rock for years. Each day, an enormous eagle ate chunks of Prometheus's liver. Every night, Prometheus's liver would grow back. The next day, he would endure the torture all over again. After thousands of years of this torture, Heracles set Prometheus free by killing the eagle.

Pandora

Prometheus was not the only one to be punished for disobeying the gods. Zeus decided to punish humans as well. This brings us to another famous Greek myth—the story of Pandora.

When Zeus set out to punish humans, he noticed that they were all alike. They were all men. He decided that there should be

In this painting, Pandora is shown opening the jar that she was forbidden to unseal. Hesiod actually linked the myths of Pandora and Prometheus. Zeus created Pandora as the price of the fire that Prometheus stole and as punishment to mankind in general. Pandora then married Epimetheus. Only later did Zeus punish Prometheus by chaining him to a rock and having an eagle pick out his liver.

women, too. Zeus and the other gods and goddesses created a human woman. Each of the gods and goddesses gave her a gift, so they named her Pandora, which means "all gifts." Athena taught her how to weave and cook. Hermes taught her how to speak well and be tricky. In addition to these gifts, Zeus gave her a large jar filled with more gifts. He told her, however, that she should never open the jar. (In some versions of the story, the gifts were stored in a box.)

With her gifts in hand, Pandora was brought by Hermes to Epimetheus (Prometheus's brother) and they got married. Pandora knew she must not open the jar, but one day her curiosity got the better of her. She decided to open the jar. Epimetheus was not that smart, and he went along with her plan, even though he knew they should not open the jar. When they took the lid off, out flew terrible things, including sickness, poverty, jealousy, and revenge. Pandora closed the jar as quickly as she could, but it was too late. All that was left in the jar was hope, which was supposed to comfort humans in the face of the evils that were now loose in the world.

There is another version of the Pandora story, written later, that says that Zeus and the other gods and goddesses gave Pandora many good things in the jar. Zeus told her not to open it, but she did not obey. In this version, all of the good things in life flew out of the jar, leaving only hope to make humans feel better.

Perseus and Medusa

There are many stories about Perseus and his bravery. One of the best known is the story of his bravery in the face of the monstrous Medusa.

Perseus was the son of Zeus and Danae, a human woman. Before Perseus was born, Danae's father had learned that

This fifth- or sixth-century-BC sculpture depicts the myth of Perseus and Medusa. Shown is Perseus *(center)* cutting off the head of Medusa, who was the most famous of all Gorgons, or monster figures of the underworld.

one day he would have a grandchild who would kill him. When Danae gave birth to Perseus, her father knew he would have to get rid of the baby. He put Perseus and Danae into a chest and set the chest in the ocean. Danae and her son floated on the ocean for days but were eventually rescued by a king named Polydectes, who took them into his home. Polydectes fell in love with Danae. He wanted to marry her, but Danae told him that she was too busy taking care of her son.

Polydectes waited until Perseus grew up, and then he came up with what he thought was the perfect plan to get rid of Perseus. With Perseus out of the picture, he would be free to marry Danae. Polydectes told Perseus to bring him the head of Medusa. Medusa was one of the Gorgons, three underworld sisters whose hair was made of live, wriggling snakes. Medusa had a beautiful face, but could turn anyone to stone with just one look.

No one believed Perseus would be able to complete this task without being turned to stone. Perseus had no idea how he would kill Medusa, but he didn't think he could refuse Polydectes' request. After all, Polydectes had taken care of him and his mother.

Perseus prayed to Athena, goddess of wisdom, for help. Athena told him exactly what to do. First, she told him, he must visit the Graeae. The Graeae were three old women who had just one eye and one tooth to share among the three of them. When he found the Graeae, Perseus stole their one eye. To get it back, the Graeae agreed to give him tools that would help him kill Medusa. They gave him Hermes' sandals, which had wings on them so that he could fly. They also gave him a bag in which to carry Medusa's head, and the cap of Hades, which would make him invisible. Athena gave him a shield that was as shiny as a mirror. Hades gave him an unbreakable sword.

Wearing the cap and carrying the other tools he had been given, Perseus approached Medusa in her cave. Knowing that he would be turned to stone with just one glance, he looked only at Medusa's reflection in his shield. He snuck up on her *and cut off her head. Still not looking at her face, he grabbed a handful of the snakes that surrounded her face. Perseus then stuffed Medusa's head into his bag.*

Using his winged sandals, Perseus flew away from Medusa's cave. As he soared over the desert, drops of Medusa's blood fell onto the sand. The blood turned into the poisonous snakes that still live in the desert today.

Returning to his home, he brought Medusa's head to Polydectes. Polydectes was surprised to see Perseus and didn't believe he had killed Medusa. Offended that Polydectes didn't believe him, Perseus held up Medusa's head. Polydectes immediately turned to stone.

Remembering the many gifts that he was given, Perseus returned them. He also gave Medusa's head to Athena. From then on, she wore it around her neck on a necklace as part of her armor.

Hermes the Trickster

Some Greek gods were known for their playfulness and trickery. Some tricked humans; others liked to trick their fellow gods and goddesses. Hermes was one such trickster.

Hermes was making mischief almost from the moment he was born. His father was Zeus, and his mother was a nymph named Maia. Hermes was born in a cave at dawn. By noon, he had grown big enough to walk. Outside the cave he discovered a turtle and scooped the turtle's body out of the shell. Across the empty shell he stretched seven strings made from sheep's gut. His new creation was the lyre, a musical instrument. After playing the lyre for a while, he was bored and ready for a new adventure.

Spotting a herd of white cattle nearby, he decided to play a trick on the owner of the cows. Hermes stole the cows, leading them away from their pasture. To disguise his tracks, he tied bundles of branches and reeds around his feet. He made the cows walk backward so the owner would not be able to follow their footprints either.

What Hermes didn't know was that the cattle belonged to his half-brother Apollo, who was also a son of Zeus. Apollo was the god of prophecy, so he knew who had stolen his cattle. He didn't know where they were, but he knew where to find Hermes.

Apollo went to the cave where Hermes had been born. There he found Hermes hiding in his cradle, pretending

The Greek god Hermes is represented here in this sixth-century-BC Etruscan bust. Hermes was generally associated with the protection of sheep and cattle. The myth of Hermes, however, portrays him as a trickster, or a deceptive and cunning character. Tricksters are prevalent throughout most, if not all, mythologies.

to be a day-old baby. By this time, he was already full grown, so Apollo didn't fall for his trick or take pity on him. Apollo demanded to know where Hermes had taken his cattle. Hermes could tell Apollo was angry and tried to calm him, still pretending to be an innocent baby.

Apollo didn't play along, but he was amused by Hermes' cleverness. He took Hermes to their father, Zeus, who ordered Hermes to return the cattle. Hermes agreed, and decided to give Apollo his lyre to make him less angry. As the god of music, Apollo was thrilled with the gift. He decided to let Hermes keep the cattle, and Zeus made Hermes the god of herds.

Phaethon

The tale of Phaethon is another example of a cautionary myth. This one warns sons to listen carefully to their fathers.

Phaethon was the son of Helios. When Phaethon was growing up, Clymene told him stories of his important father. She told him how Apollo drove the golden chariot of the sun across the sky each day.

Phaethon was proud of his father's important task. When one of his friends said he didn't believe that Apollo was Phaethon's father, Phaethon decided to prove it. His mother told him to go east, to where the sun rose in the sky. There he would meet Apollo.

Phaethon set out to visit his father's golden palace. When Phaethon arrived, Apollo greeted him happily because he

This eighteenth-century ceramic carving depicts the myth of Phaethon. Illustrated is Phaethon at the reigns of the chariot of his father, Apollo. True to Apollo's prediction, Phaethon didn't have the skill to maintain control over the chariot and its horses, and he eventually perished.

recognized Phaethon as his son. Apollo asked him why he had come. Phaethon replied that he had come to get proof that Apollo was his father. Apollo assured him that he was his father and he granted Phaethon one wish. Phaethon didn't even need to think about what his one wish would be. Immediately, he asked Apollo if he could drive Apollo's golden chariot for one day.

Apollo knew that if he granted this wish it would end in disaster for Phaethon. He tried to persuade Phaethon to make another wish. He told him how difficult it would be for him to drive the horses that pulled the chariot. He explained that the climb into the sky was very steep and Phaethon could fall out *of the chariot. Or he might get dizzy being so high in the sky. Apollo begged Phaethon to make a different wish.*

Phaethon was brave, though, and foolish. Apollo could tell he would not be able to change Phaethon's mind, so he agreed to grant Phaethon's wish. Phaethon climbed into the golden chariot and took the reins of the fire-breathing horses. They set out on their path through the heavens, bringing light to the eastern sky. However, the horses quickly realized that the chariot was not as heavy as it usually was. They knew Apollo was not driving them and soon they were out of control. Phaethon was not strong enough to get them back on the right path and they began to fall to Earth. The heat from the chariot baked the earth beneath it, turning the land into a desert. It also burned the skin of the people living in the land below, turning it black.

To save the earth from more destruction, Zeus threw a thunderbolt at Phaethon. The heat from the thunderbolt set Phaethon's hair on fire and Phaethon plunged to earth, looking like a shooting star. Phaethon fell into a river, where he died.

What We Learn from These Myths

The stories of Narcissus, Pandora, and Phaethon are examples of warning myths. Narcissus illustrated the importance of being aware of others besides one's self. Pandora's story also reminded humans of the terrible things that can happen if they did not obey the gods and goddesses. The myth of Phaethon is a cautionary tale about listening to elders.

The myths of Narcissus, Prometheus, Phaethon, and Hermes all taught other lessons to the Greeks. Prometheus's story described the origin of fire and how humans came to be. The Phaethon myth illustrated how the sun moves across the sky and why it rises in the east. It accounts for why the desert is so hot and dry and why people living there have dark skin. Phaethon's fall to Earth also offered an explanation for shooting stars. The story of Hermes is an example of a myth that describes what the gods were like. It also tells how the lyre was created. The Perseus myth is just one example of heroic adventure. It tells the story of a brave human helped by the gods and goddesses.

While these myths may not be tales of events that we think could actually happen, they cover things we can all relate to and understand. They tell stories of pride, persistence, courage, jealousy, and curiosity.

Greek Mythology in Our Lives Today

Although the Greek myths were originally told thousands of years ago, they have remained an important part of our lives. Over the years, since they were first written, the way people interpret them has changed.

Originally, myths also explained natural phenomena such as earthquakes or lightning. As the Greeks learned more about science, they found other reasons for these natural occurrences. This

The Temple of Athena Nike, shown here, is one of the many ancient Greek ruins that we continue to appreciate and learn from today. This temple was built in the fifth century BC and sits beside the gateway to the Acropolis in Athens.

made myths seem less important or believable as explanations.

However, myths remain important because they tell stories about events and emotions that everyone experiences. People today still feel anger, love, and jealousy just as the Greeks did. The myths are also exciting and filled with adventure—they are just plain good stories.

Artists and writers have used Greek myths as inspiration for their works for thousands of years. They have painted scenes from the myths or based plays on stories told by the Greeks. Composers have written operas based on myths, and stories have been retold in modern novels.

The Greek myths continue to be part of our everyday lives. Some famous expressions come from Greek myths, such as "Pandora's box." Pandora's story is told as a warning to people to be careful about their actions, as they can have serious negative consequences. There are television shows, movies, and video games based on the adventures of Heracles. Movies based on Greek myths include *Clash of the Titans* (1981) and *Troy* (2004). Characters from Greek myths are also used in advertising. The Greek god Hermes, with his winged cap and shoes, is used by delivery services, such as FTD, the flower delivery company.

Greek myths have been told and retold since the earliest days of civilization. Their tales of excitement and emotions are sure to live on for years to come.

GLOSSARY

chariot A two-wheeled, horse-drawn vehicle of ancient times used in battle and also in races and parades.

city-state A self-governing state consisting of a city and surrounding territory.

discus A heavy disk that is thrown as far as possible in an athletic competition.

fertile Being able to procreate, particularly fruit and other crops.

fleet A group of ships, which sail together.

hospitality Friendly treatment to guests.

literal True, or following the exact meaning.

mosaic A decoration on a surface made by setting small pieces of glass or stone of different colors on a surface to create pictures or patterns.

pasture A plot of land where animals are allowed to graze.

pillar A column that supports a roof or ceiling.

pomegranate A reddish fruit about the size of an orange that has a thick skin and many edible seeds.

prophecy A prediction of the future.

ritual A formal ceremony.

sacrifice The act of offering something precious to a god.

temple A building for religious worship.

FOR MORE INFORMATION

The Ancient Greek World
University of Pennsylvania Museum of Archaeology
   and Anthropology
3260 South Street
Philadelphia, PA 19104
(215) 898-4000
Web site: http://www.museum.upenn.edu/Greek_World/index2.html

Department of Greek and Roman Studies
University of Victoria
P.O. Box 1700 STN CSC
Victoria, British Columbia V8W 2Y2
Canada
(250) 721-7211
Web site: http://web.uvic.ca/grs/bowman/myth

History for Kids
Portland State University
Portland, OR 97207
Web site: http://www.historyforkids.org

The Perseus Digital Library
Tufts University
Medford, MA 02155
Web site: http://www.perseus.tufts.edu

Web Sites

Due to the changing nature of Internet links, the Rosen Publishing Group, Inc., has developed an online list of Web sites related to the subject of this book. This site is updated regularly. Please use this link to access the list:

http://www.rosenlinks.com/maw/gree

FOR FURTHER READING

Bolton, Leslie. *The Everything Classical Mythology Book: Greek and Roman Gods, Goddesses, Heroes, and Monsters from Ares to Zeus.* Avon, MA: Adams Media Corporation, 2002.

Coolidge, Olivia. *Greek Myths.* Boston, MA: Houghton Mifflin Company, 2001.

Evslin, Bernard. *Heroes, Gods and Monsters of the Greek Myths.* New York, NY: Laurel Leaf, 1984.

Gibson, Michael. *Gods, Men, and Monsters from the Greek Myths.* New York, NY: Peter Bedrick Books, 1991.

Nardo, Don. *Greek and Roman Mythology.* San Diego, CA: Lucent Books, 1998.

Nardo, Don. *Heroes: Discovering Mythology.* San Diego, CA: Lucent Books, 2002.

Nardo, Don. *Living in Ancient Greece.* San Diego, CA: Greenhaven Press, 2004.

BIBLIOGRAPHY

Buxton, Richard. *The Complete World of Greek Mythology*. London, England: Thames and Hudson, 2004.

Campbell, Joseph. *Creative Mythology: The Masks of God*. New York, NY: Penguin Books, 1968.

Coolidge, Olivia. *Greek Myths*. Boston, MA: Houghton Mifflin Company, 1977.

Eddy, Steve, and Claire Hamilton. *Greek Myths*. Lincolnwood, IL: Contemporary Books, 2001.

Gibson, Michael. *Gods, Men, and Monsters from the Greek Myths*. New York, NY: Peter Bedrick Books, 1991.

Graves, Robert. *The Greek Myths: Complete Edition*. London, England: Penguin Books, 1992.

Leeming, David Adams. *Mythology: The Voyage of the Hero*. New York, NY: Oxford University Press, 1998.

Lefkowitz, Mary. *Greek Gods, Human Lives: What We Can Learn from Myths*. New Haven, CT: Yale University Press, 2003.

Morford, Mark P. O., and Robert J. Lenardon. *Classical Mythology*, Seventh Ed. New York, NY: Oxford University Press, 2002.

Nardo, Don. *Greek and Roman Mythology*. San Diego, CA: Lucent Books, 1998.

Nardo, Don. *Heroes: Discovering Mythology*. San Diego, CA: Lucent Books, 2002.

Nardo, Don. *Living in Ancient Greece*. San Diego, CA: Greenhaven Press, 2004.

◼ INDEX

About the Author

Simone Payment has a degree in psychology from Cornell University and a master's degree in elementary education from Wheelock College. She is the author of eleven books for young adults. Her book *Inside Special Operations: Navy SEALs* (also from Rosen Publishing) won a 2004 Quick Picks for Reluctant Young Readers award from the American Library Association and is on the Nonfiction Honor List of Voice of Youth Advocates.

Photo Credits

Cover, p. 1 © The Art Archive/Nation Archaeological Museum Athens/Dagli Orti; pp. 4–5, 9, 11 (inset), 13 (bottom), 21, 22, 31, 33, 36, 38, 40, 41, 50, 52 © The Bridgeman Art Library; p. 8, 18, 19, 24 © Erich Lessing/Art Resource, NY; p. 10 © Nimatallah/Art Resource, NY; p. 11 © Robert Gill, Papilio/Corbis; p. 12 © SEF/Art Resource, NY; p. 13 (top) courtesy of the Reading University Library; p. 14 Araldo de Luca/Corbis; p. 16 © Giraudon/Art Resource, NY; p. 20 © Mary Evans Picture Library; p. 25 © The Art Archive/Bardo Museum Tunis; p. 27 © Vanni/Art Resource, NY; p. 28 © The Art Archive/Museo Statale Metaponto/Dagli Orti; pp. 29, 34 © The Art Archive/Museo Nazionale Palazzo Altemps Rome/Dagli Orti; p. 43 © Philadelphia Museum of Art/Corbis; p. 45 © Cameraphoto Arte, Venice/Art Resource, NY; p. 47 © The Art Archive/National Museum Palermo/Dagli Orti; p. 55 © The Art Archive/Dagli Orti.

Designer: Thomas Forget; Editor: Nicholas Croce
Photo Researcher: Hillary Arnold